Date: 9/19/17

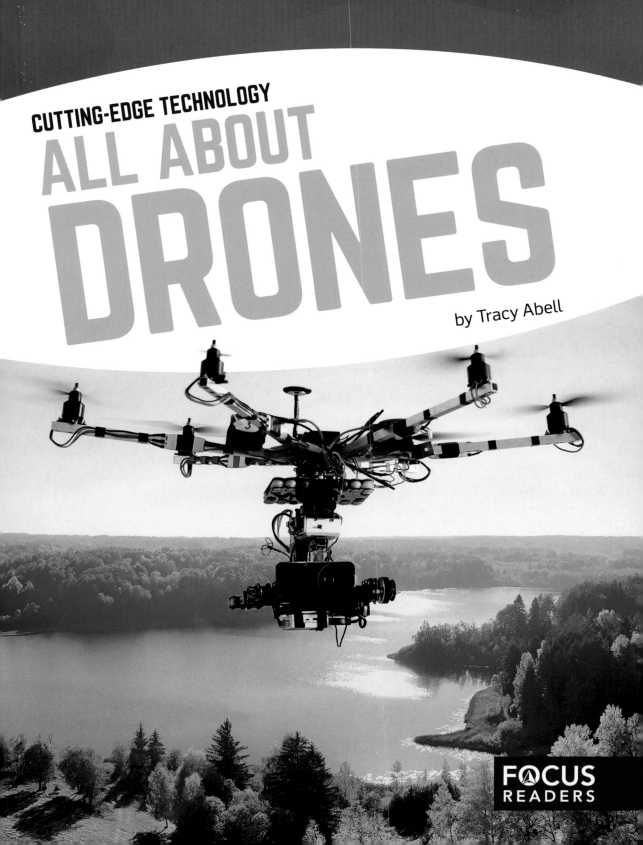

CUTTING-EDGE TECHNOLOGY

ALL ABOUT
DRONES

by Tracy Abell

FOCUS
READERS

WWW.NORTHSTAREDITIONS.COM

Produced for North Star Editions by Red Line Editorial.

Photographs ©: Alexey Yuzhakov/Shutterstock Images, cover, 1; Lucky Business/Shutterstock Images, 4–5; Lt. Col. Leslie Pratt/US Air Force, 6; Dmitry Kalinovsky/Shutterstock Images, 9; Maria Dryfhout/Shutterstock Images, 10–11; seregalsv/Shutterstock Images, 13; sezer66/iStockphoto, 15; Julia Tim/Shutterstock Images, 16–17; Kletr/Shutterstock Images, 18–19; Kike Calvo/AP Images, 21; leungchopan/Shutterstock Images, 22–23; Ververidis Vasilis/Shutterstock Images, 25; gualtiero boffi/Shutterstock Images, 26–27; Fotos593/Shutterstock Images, 29

Content Consultant: Dr. John B. Bridewell, Professor of Aviation, University of North Dakota

ISBN
978-1-63517-012-2 (hardcover)
978-1-63517-068-9 (paperback)
978-1-63517-173-0 (ebook pdf)
978-1-63517-123-5 (hosted ebook)

Library of Congress Control Number: 2016949757

Printed in the United States of America
Mankato, MN
November, 2016

ABOUT THE AUTHOR

Tracy Abell lives in the Rocky Mountain foothills where she enjoys running on the trails. She often sees coyotes, foxes, rabbits, magpies, and meadowlarks out there in the open space.

TABLE OF CONTENTS

CHAPTER 1

WHAT IS A DRONE?

You look down at a snow-covered mountain. Like an eagle, you swoop close to a lone snowboarder going down the slope. White powder sprays behind the board. Trees pass by in a green blur. You see it all: the snowboarder, the sparkling slope, and the blue sky.

Drones enable users to record events and views from exciting places and angles.

A US military drone flies a combat mission in Afghanistan.

How is this possible? You are controlling a drone that flies just above the snowboarder. The snowboarder ends her run in a powdery swoosh. The drone flies back up the mountain to you.

A drone is an aircraft that can fly without a human pilot on board. Drones come in a variety of sizes and prices. The US Air Force has many large drones. They weigh thousands of pounds and can fly more than 50,000 feet (15,240 m) above the ground.

RADIOPLANE OQ-2A

The Radioplane OQ-2A was a remote-controlled target drone flown in 1943. It had to be launched by a catapult. The OQ-2A had a wingspan of 13 feet (4.0 m) and weighed 108 pounds (49 kg). The OQ-2A could fly 8,000 feet (2,400 m) high. A Radioplane OQ-2A is on display at the National Museum of the United States Air Force in Dayton, Ohio.

These drones cost millions of dollars. Some microdrones may weigh only 1 ounce (28 g) and cost less than $100. Larger drones are typically built by manufacturers. But there are also do-it-yourself kits for building your own drone.

It is impossible to say when the first drone was invented. Some believe it was in 1849. In that year, Austria used balloons filled with bombs during a war. Others say the first drone was invented in the 1930s. That is when the United States first sent up remote-controlled aircraft. These devices were practice targets for the army.

Inexpensive hobby drones are available at many stores and online retailers.

Drones may have begun with the military. But by the 1940s, things changed. Remote-controlled aircraft became a hobby for civilians. Today, more than one million people own hobby drones.

CHAPTER 2

HOW DRONES WORK

Hobby drones come in three categories. The first is planes and gliders. These drones look like a typical piloted aircraft with two wings and a tail. They can only move forward. They cannot **hover**. Propellers are usually pointed horizontally.

Multicopters are the most popular type of drone.

The second category is helicopters. Helicopters have propellers or rotors pointed vertically. These drones can move forward, backward, and side to side. They can also hover.

The third category is multicopters. These drones typically have three to eight rotors. Multicopters move like helicopters.

All drones must be able to get up in the air. Lift is what makes objects that are heavier than air stay **aloft**. Lift happens when air is moved across wings and rotors. The upper surface is curved, and this makes the air move faster. Faster-moving air results in low pressure,

Drones carrying cameras sometimes have six to eight rotors.

which creates lift. Heavier aircraft require greater lift.

Once the drone is in the air, it needs instructions on what to do.

To control the drone, a pilot sends commands by radio frequency to the aircraft. **GPS** technology helps the drone navigate.

Radio frequency communication requires a wireless connection by means of **radio waves**. A drone and its control device are matched together and recognize each other.

Wi-Fi is a wireless Internet connection that uses radio waves. Wi-Fi also allows drones to send live video to computers, tablets, and smartphones.

GPS is mainly used to guide the drone in flight. A pilot programs the **mission** of a drone before the flight. The pilot puts in

A drone's Wi-Fi range is approximately 650 yards (600 m).

GPS **coordinates**. The drone flies to the programmed locations, gathers data, and then flies back again.

ROLL, PITCH, YAW, AND THROTTLE

Roll tilts the drone left or right. This happens by speeding up the rotors on one side and slowing down the rotors on the other side.

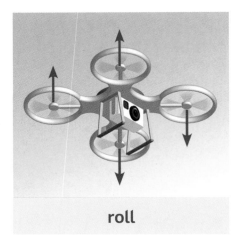

roll

Pitch tilts the drone forward or backward. This works in a similar way as roll. However, the front and back propellers are the ones that speed up or slow down rather than the propellers on the side.

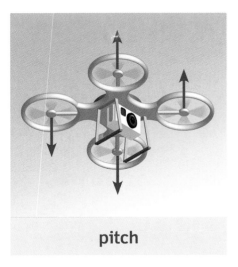

pitch

Yaw rotates the nose of the drone left or right. This happens by speeding up the rotors spinning in one direction and slowing down the rotors spinning in the opposite direction.

yaw

Throttle controls the drone's up-and-down movement. This happens by changing the speed of the rotors all at the same time.

throttle

CHAPTER 3

DRONES IN ACTION

Drones are most often used for **surveillance**. The military uses spy drones to watch what is happening on the ground. Police use drones to catch speeders.

Drones can reach places that are difficult or dangerous for humans. They go up on roofs to check for hail damage.

Farmers use drones to monitor crops for diseases, weeds, and moisture content.

19

Drones help movie directors get tricky overhead shots. In 2014, camera drones were used for the first time during the Olympics. They recorded the freestyle skiers and snowboarders. Drones are also valuable tools during emergencies. They delivered small aid packages after

DRONES IN SCHOOLS

Drones may someday become a common teaching tool. Students might take classes on how to build drones. They could learn to program drones to fly through obstacle courses. Drones could provide band directors with **aerial** views of marching band formations. Coaches might use drones to record teams running drills. Drones could even help create an end-of-year school celebration video.

Drone technology was used in Nepal after a deadly earthquake in 2015.

Haiti's 2010 earthquake. Drones may someday help deliver donated blood where it is needed.

CHAPTER 4

POTENTIAL PROBLEMS

A Federal Aviation Administration (FAA) rule restricts drones from flying within 5 miles (8.0 km) of an airport. This is because people in piloted aircraft have difficulty seeing drones. Users of small drones must be careful to stay out of the way of these aircraft.

Drone pilots must stay away from airports.

But every year, the FAA receives hundreds of reports of drones close to planes.

Drones can also cause problems for firefighters. In 2015, drones flew above a California wildfire. Helicopters were ready to take off with water buckets to put out the blaze. But the helicopters were

DEBATING DRONES

Most people agree that drones are helpful during natural disasters. And many people enjoy watching the videos drones record at sporting events. But lots of people do not want drones invading their privacy. They don't like the idea that drones could take pictures or videos of them. Some believe it is wrong to use drones in war. Drone technology has inspired strong opinions and ongoing debate.

Drones can provide beautiful shots from high above stadiums.

delayed for several minutes. The pilots had to wait until they were sure the area was clear of drones.

Drones can also cause animals stress. A study confirmed that black bears' heart rates increased when they saw drones. Some birds abandon their nests if drones get too close.

CHAPTER 5

THE FUTURE OF DRONES

Drones offer many potential uses. Amazon Prime Air may someday use drones to deliver packages to customers in 30 minutes. A golf course in Japan is testing the drone delivery of drinks and balls to golfers.

Designers are also working to create new search-and-rescue drones.

Delivery drones may be common in the future.

These tiny drones would be sent into buildings after fires and explosions. They would work as a team to check for survivors and map out the building. The drones would also record the temperature and air quality. This information would help rescue workers stay safe.

Drone technology is changing quickly. Designers continue to make drones that go farther and faster. As more drones take to the sky, the need for **regulations** will grow. The FAA continues to work on new rules. In the meantime, state governments are already passing laws for drones. The FAA also has a smartphone app called B4UFLY. This app helps drone

Engineers continue to work on drones that can be used in disasters such as earthquakes.

users make sure they are flying in an unrestricted area. As drones become a more common sight in our skies, these rules will help keep pilots and people on the ground safe.

FOCUS ON
DRONES

Write your answers on a separate piece of paper.

1. Write a sentence summarizing the main idea of Chapter 3.

2. Do you think the FAA should make stricter rules about drones? Why or why not?

3. Which type of drone typically has three to eight rotors?
    - **A.** gliders
    - **B.** helicopters
    - **C.** multicopters

4. What problem might occur if a small drone flew near an airport?
    - **A.** Airplane pilots would not be able to see the drone.
    - **B.** The drone would interfere with the airport's Wi-Fi.
    - **C.** The drone would not be able to generate enough lift.

Answer key on page 32.

GLOSSARY

aerial
Taking place in the air.

aloft
Up in the air.

coordinates
A set of longitude and latitude numbers used to find a location.

GPS
Short for "global positioning system," a navigation system that uses satellites to figure out location.

hover
To stay in one place in the air.

mission
The reason a drone is flying.

radio waves
Electromagnetic waves used to transmit signals for radio and television.

regulations
Official laws about how something should be done.

surveillance
The act of watching an area closely.

TO LEARN MORE

BOOKS

Dougherty, Martin J. *Drones: An Illustrated Guide to the Unmanned Aircraft That Are Filling Our Skies*. London: Amber Books, 2015.

Faust, Daniel R. *Entertainment Drones*. New York: PowerKids Press, 2016.

Rose, Simon. *Drones*. New York: AV2 by Weigl, 2014.

NOTE TO EDUCATORS

Visit **www.focusreaders.com** to find lesson plans, activities, links, and other resources related to this title.

INDEX

Answer Key: 1. Answers will vary; **2.** Answers will vary; **3.** C; **4.** A